THERE IS BEAUTY HERE

There Is Beauty Here

Finding Joy After Failure

A One-Month Devotional

REBECCA BOLIN

RESOURCE *Publications* · Eugene, Oregon

THERE IS BEAUTY HERE
Finding Joy After Failure

Copyright © 2019 Rebecca Bolin. All rights reserved. Except for brief quotations in critical publications or reviews, no part of this book may be reproduced in any manner without prior written permission from the publisher. Write: Permissions, Wipf and Stock Publishers, 199 W. 8th Ave., Suite 3, Eugene, OR 97401.

Resource Publications
An Imprint of Wipf and Stock Publishers
199 W. 8th Ave., Suite 3
Eugene, OR 97401

www.wipfandstock.com

PAPERBACK ISBN: 978-1-5326-8709-9
HARDCOVER ISBN: 978-1-5326-8710-5
EBOOK ISBN: 978-1-5326-8711-2

Manufactured in the U.S.A.   JUNE 14, 2019

Scripture quotations marked (NIV) are taken from the Holy Bible, New International Version®, NIV®. Copyright © 1973, 1978, 1984, 2011 by Biblica, Inc.™ Used by permission of Zondervan. All rights reserved worldwide. www.zondervan.com The "NIV" and "New International Version" are trademarks registered in the United States Patent and Trademark Office by Biblica, Inc.™

Scripture quotations taken from the New American Standard Bible® (NASB), Copyright © 1960, 1962, 1963, 1968, 1971, 1972, 1973, 1975, 1977, 1995 by The Lockman Foundation Used by permission. www.Lockman.org

This devotional is dedicated to Pastor Brad, a man of integrity, who still hears from God, and who is not afraid to change his sermon at the last minute to deliver the message that God Almighty has planted in his heart.

Contents

Acknowledgments | ix
Abbreviations | xi
Introduction | xiii

There is Beauty Here, Day 1 | 1
There is Beauty in the Way He Cares for His Creation, Day 2 | 3
There is Beauty in Redemption, Day 3 | 5
There is Beauty in the Battle, Day 4 | 7
There is Beauty in Confession, Day 5 | 10
There is Beauty in Correction, Day 6 | 12
There is Beauty in Blessing, Day 7 | 14
There is Beauty in Restoration, Day 8 | 17
There is Beauty in Reconciliation, Day 9 | 19
There is Beauty in Our Weakness and Imperfection, Day 10 | 21
There is Beauty in Persistence, Day 11 | 23
There is Beauty in Obedience, Day 12 | 25
There is Beauty in Fellowship, Day 13 | 27
There is Beauty in Trust: Overcoming Guilt (Part 1), Day 14 | 29
There is Beauty in Praise: Overcoming Guilt (Part 2), Day 15 | 31
Finding Joy: Forgive Others Unconditionally, Day 16 | 33
Finding Joy: Forgive Yourself, Day 17 | 35
Finding Joy: Embrace Healing, Day 18 | 38
Finding Joy: Think Positively, Day 19 | 40
Finding Joy: Renew Daily, Day 20 | 42
Finding Joy: Practice Discretion, Day 21 | 44

Finding Joy: Meditate on God's Word (Part 1), Day 22 | 46
Finding Joy: Meditate on God's Word (Part 2), Day 23 | 48
Finding Joy: Let Go of Injustice, Day 24 | 50
Finding Joy: Seek Diligently, Day 25 | 52
Finding Joy: Spread the Light, Day 26 | 54
Finding Joy: Judge Not, Day 27 | 56
Finding Joy: Claim God's Promises, Day 28 | 58
Finding Joy: Give Generously, Day 29 | 60
Finding Joy: Live Harmoniously, Day 30 | 62
Finding Joy: Love Abundantly, Day 31 | 64
Final Thoughts | 66

Acknowledgments

PRAISE BE TO ALMIGHTY God for giving me the courage and inspiration to create and share this work. To Lacey, my daughter and loyal friend, whose instincts and wisdom I trust and greatly respect, thank you for being my first reader and for your valuable edits and insights. To my husband, Bill, who first encouraged me to write, thank you for your confidence, your fine eye for detail, and for your steadfast support; I am truly grateful.

Abbreviations

MOST OF THE SCRIPTURES cited in this work are from the King James translation of the Bible; however, is some instances, other translations of the Bible are referenced. Please see the list below for the abbreviations used in this text.

KJV   King James Version
NASB   New American Standard Bible
NIV   New International Version

Introduction

MANY OF US ARE familiar with the stages of grief when we lose a loved one. Our hearts are sorrowful, and we must find a way to cope with the emotions that threaten to consume us. Other events, such as divorce, can trigger similar patterns in our lives. For the Christian, the realization that we have failed God, our loving heavenly father, and wounded those we love can launch a cycle of grief, guilt, remorse, depression, and self-doubt that can become spiritually crippling if we allow it to consume us. We know God forgives, but how do we forgive ourselves and let go of the grief and pain we have caused? How do we achieve spiritual freedom from the chains of condemnation the enemy desires to keep fastened upon us?

Although the process is not easy, there is healing and restoration from the knowledge and pain of failure. There is a soothing balm for the guilt and remorse that rise up against us, and it is found in the word of God and in spending time with our savior. All the answers we need are plainly given to those who seek him with a broken heart and contrite spirit. We can learn to accept, and yes, love the new person we have become through the faithfulness and provision of our loving heavenly father. The journey begins with learning to see ourselves the way God sees us.

I would like for readers of this devotional to know that I approach the writing of this work with complete humility and awareness of my sin before God. Romans 2:10 teaches, "For all have sinned, and come short of the glory of God (KJV). There is not one of us who has attained perfection in our spiritual walk; only Christ was able to achieve that. Yet, some of us seem to really miss the mark and commit sins that leave ourselves and others broken and hurting. I was one of those people. I can relate to Paul who

INTRODUCTION

states in 1 Timothy 1:15, "This is a faithful saying, and worthy of all acceptation, that Christ Jesus came into the world to save sinners; of whom I am chief" (KJV). I recognized my sin, my shortcomings, and my absolute need for the atoning blood of Jesus to cover my transgressions and cleanse me from all unrighteousness. Even though I prayed earnestly and often for forgiveness for my own failures, I struggled for years with guilt, depression and deep remorse. I punished myself by refusing opportunities to minister and touch others, and I questioned whether or not I was truly forgiven. I isolated myself from those around me and thought I was not worthy to be used by God. By searching the Bible and writing down every detail of what God revealed to me through the scriptures, I gradually came to appreciate and embrace the unfailing love and boundless mercy of our heavenly father; I was able to release the pain and, finally, forgive myself.

This devotional is a compilation of that time spent with the Lord, reading his word, meditating upon it, praying, and listening to his voice. My deepest and most sincere prayer is that you will find refuge, help, comfort, peace, and healing as you read these words and search the scriptures with me. May God's blessings rest upon each of you.

There is Beauty Here
Day 1

"But now, O Lord, thou art our father; we are the clay, and thou our potter; and we all are the work of thy hand"
—ISA 64:8 KJV

WE ARE ALL LIKE lumps of clay in the hands of a loving God. There is beauty in the way he pulls us up from the miry pit and shapes us into a fine vessel that is ready for service. God takes all of our dirt and filth and clothes us in his righteousness. Even when we go through correction, hardship, pain, and disappointment there is beauty in the way God puts us back on the wheel and molds us and shapes us into a work of art that is pleasing to him. He keeps working the clay and fashions us into an instrument that can be used by him. He smooths out the rough edges and fires us in trials that test the limits of our strength and yet, somehow, make us even stronger. Sometimes, he even crushes us and starts over, but he never throws us away. He is the master creator, and we are his handiwork. His discipline can be hard, but he guides us through his living word. When we heed his word, he speaks to us through it, and reveals the areas where we need to be refined. There is beauty in the work he is doing. There is beauty in the time he takes to get our attention and correct us. There is beauty in the way he orchestrates our lives to place us in contact with people who speak light and life to us. There is beauty in the way he defines our path—how he laid it out from the very beginning to give us every opportunity to grow and make right choices. There is beauty in the way he inhabits our praises (Ps. 22:3). When we praise him, his presence is right there with us, and we can feel him near. There is beauty in the way he meets us in our quiet moments of prayer and calms our fears and anxieties. There is beauty in the way he responds to his children with comfort and strength when we cry to him for help. There is beauty in the way he teaches us to trust in him—to believe that he really is working all things together for our good (Rom 8:28). And there is beauty in the way he embraces us and washes over us in a flood of joy when we give with no thought of receiving. His unfailing love for us is beautiful and it is beyond comprehension. His love has no bounds. It has no beginning, and it has no end. He is from everlasting to everlasting, and he is reaching out his hand to us. All we have to do is accept his beautiful gift.

Prayer

Lord, help me to understand that you love me with an unfailing love. Your mercy and your goodness endure forever. Help me to believe that if I confess my sins to you, you are faithful and just to forgive me of my sin and to cleanse me from all unrighteousness (1 John 1:9), not because of *my* goodness or anything I have done to earn your forgiveness, but because of *your* goodness and great mercy.

There is Beauty in the Way He Cares for His Creation

Day 2

"Now the tax collectors and sinners were all gathering around to hear Jesus. But the Pharisees and the teachers of the law muttered, "This man welcomes sinners and eats with them." Then Jesus told them this parable: "Suppose one of you has a hundred sheep and loses one of them. Doesn't he leave the ninety-nine in the open country and go after the lost sheep until he finds it? And when he finds it, he joyfully puts it on his shoulders and goes home. Then he calls his friends and neighbors together and says, 'Rejoice with me; I have found my lost sheep.' I tell you that in the same way there will be more rejoicing in heaven over one sinner who repents than over ninety-nine righteous persons who do not need to repent"

—LUKE 15:1–7 NIV

DON'T YOU FIND IT interesting that there is more rejoicing in heaven over the one lost sheep that is found than over ninety-nine that never strayed? Why is that? Isn't it more admirable to stay close to the shepherd and always be obedient and follow close to him? Jesus uses this parable to demonstrate his unfailing love for us. Who among us can relate to the ninety-nine? Which one of us can say that we have *never* sinned or strayed from the shepherd? God in his infinite wisdom knows that each of us has wandered from the fold and lost contact with the sound of his voice. He knows that we can relate best to the one lost sheep because we *are* that sheep. Each of us has fallen short at times, but God does not leave us alone in the wilderness to die in our sin. He comes after us because he loves us and does not want to see us perish. (See Luke 19:10). He leaves the ninety-nine, knowing they are safe and will remain faithful, and he searches for the lost sheep and finds it (us). He brings us back safely into the fold and rejoices over us along with the hosts of heaven.

To further extend the metaphor of the sheep, we move to John 10:27–28 (KJV). Jesus says: "My sheep hear my voice, and I know them, and they follow me: And I give unto them eternal life; and they shall never perish, neither shall any man pluck them out of my hand." God has expectations that we follow him. He does not expect to continually leave the fold to go searching for the same lost sheep. If we stray, he will come after us, but he desires for us to know his voice and to stay close to him. We achieve that closeness by maturing in the word and spending time with our Lord so that we recognize his voice and obey him. When we know the shepherd's voice, we will not be led astray or distracted by others. When we stay close to the Lord, we cannot be deceived or enticed by any trick of the enemy. No man will be able to "pluck" us from the hand of the father.

Prayer

Dear Lord, please help me to hear and know your voice and to stay close to you. Thank you for the times that you have come searching for me and delivered me from the snares of the enemy. Thank you for the times you have brought me back to the safety and security of your fold. Help me now, Lord, to remain faithful and strong and show others the way to you.

There is Beauty in Redemption
Day 3

"[For] all have sinned and fall short of the glory of God, and all are justified freely by his grace through the redemption that came by Christ Jesus"

—ROM 3:23–24 NIV

THE WORD OF GOD tells us plainly that we have all sinned and fallen short of the glory of God. As humans, there is no way we can measure up to God's standard of perfection, yet Jesus Christ, being God (and man) on earth, was able to fulfill that objective. He lived a perfect life and paid the penalty for our sin through his death on the cross. He took the shame and punishment we deserve. He conquered sin and death, and by believing in him and turning from our sins, we, too, can have eternal life. When we accept Christ's forgiveness, he redeems us and sets us free from the chains of sin and death.

So why do we find it so hard to forgive ourselves? Why do we revisit our past and question whether or not we are truly forgiven? It is, perhaps, because that in our humanity, we cannot truly fathom the kind of love that does not keep a record of wrongdoing, that does not dredge up the past and hold it over the head of the evildoer. We must understand that when we go back in our minds and relive our past faults and failures and question God's forgiveness, we take value away from what Christ did for us. In our minds we minimize the sacrifice Jesus made. We try to make God smaller than what he is, who he is. We try to fit him into our limited concept of love and forgiveness.

We have to understand that our forgiveness is finished. There is nothing else that needs to be done. Psalm 103:12 explains that God has removed our transgressions "as far as the east is from the west" (NIV). It is over. We have to let go of our mistakes and embrace the mercy and forgiveness God has extended to us. When the enemy tries to remind us of our failures, and we feel engulfed by waves of guilt and shame, we can turn to the scriptures that remind us of what Christ has done for us. When we begin to truly fathom the love of God and the extent of his forgiveness, we can begin to find true joy and walk in the victory God desires for us. (See also 1 John 3:20.)

Prayer

Dear Lord, thank you for the sacrifice of Jesus Christ on the cross for my sins. Help me to understand your great love and mercy for me. Help me, by faith, to embrace the forgiveness you have extended to me and to forgive myself. Help me to let go of the past and walk in the joy of your salvation.

There is Beauty in the Battle
Day 4

"Wherefore take unto you the whole armour of God, that ye may be able to withstand in the evil day, and having done all, to stand. Stand therefore, having your loins girt about with truth, and having on the breastplate of righteousness; And your feet shod with the preparation of the gospel of peace; Above all, taking the shield of faith, wherewith ye shall be able to quench all the fiery darts of the wicked. And take the helmet of salvation, and the sword of the Spirit, which is the word of God: Praying always with all prayer and supplication in the Spirit, and watching thereunto with all perseverance and supplication for all saints"

—EPH 6:13-18 KJV).

LETTING GO OF PAIN, past offenses, guilt, and fear frees us to pursue God. He has an abundant life in store for us, but we will not enjoy it fully if we are held prisoner by the past or by fear. The enemy has a way of planting thoughts in our mind to keep us bound by those emotions, but God has provided a way for us to be victorious. He instructs us in his word to be clothed with the whole armor of God. This is the key to being armed and ready when unwanted thoughts try to creep in. The armor of God protects the entire body and the mind. We need faith that the word of God is true and to believe that he will do what he says he will do. We need to have accepted God's plan for salvation and be clothed in his righteousness and truth. We need to live peaceably with those around us, avoiding strife and contention. We need to stay close to the Lord through prayer and through the reading of his word. Every part of the armor is for our defense, our protection, except the sword. The sword is an offensive weapon. God places his word in our hands and in our hearts, so that we can wage battle against the enemy. When those painful thoughts come, it is the word of God that drives back the enemy. Some examples from the scriptures are the following:

> "For God hath not given us the spirit of fear; but of power, and of love, and of a sound mind (2 Tim 1:7 KJV).
>
> "So shall they fear the name of the Lord from the west, and his glory from the rising of the sun. When the enemy shall come in like a flood, the Spirit of the Lord shall lift up a standard against him" (Isa 59:19 KJV).
>
> "What shall we then say to these things? If God be for us, who can be against us?" (Rom 8:31 KJV).
>
> "Nay, in all these things we are more than conquerors through him that loved us. For I am persuaded, that neither death, nor life, nor angels, nor principalities, nor powers, nor things present, nor things to come, nor height, nor depth, nor any other creature, shall be able to separate us from the love of God, which is in Christ Jesus our Lord" (Rom 8:37–39 KJV).

There are many other scriptures God has provided for spiritual warfare, but if we are not reading his word and hiding it in our hearts, we will not have that spiritual sword ready when the enemy attacks. Staying full of the word of God is one of the most effective ways we can overcome negative thoughts and protect our minds and our hearts from the pain, fear, and guilt of the past.

Prayer

Dear Lord, please help me to stay close to you and remain armed and ready for whatever comes my way. Help me to hide your word in my heart so that I may find comfort, peace, and strength in this powerful gift you have given me. Help me to discipline myself to know your word, so that I may draw strength from it in the moment when it is needed.

There is Beauty in Confession
Day 5

"Confess your faults one to another, and pray one for another, that ye may be healed. The effectual fervent prayer of a righteous man availeth much"

—JAS 5:16 KJV

IF YOU ARE STRUGGLING with a particular sin in your life or even just the temptation to sin, strength and healing can be found in confession. We are often reluctant to admit to others that we are struggling with temptation or that we have failed God. We may be embarrassed or feel that others are growing more quickly in their walk. We may want to project the image that we have it all together. Whatever holds us back from confessing our shortcomings is keeping us in bondage and stunting our spiritual growth. As long as we nurture even a tiny root of that sin in our hearts, it can spring back to life. It is one of the enemy's favorite tricks for killing our joy.

If you want to be truly set free from that thing that is harassing and oppressing you, confess those hidden sins to someone you trust and ask that person to pray with you and for you. In other words, don't just talk about it; make it a matter of serious prayer. God placed us among other Christians so that we may draw strength and support from each other. Confession enables you to get that sin out in the open and you essentially make yourself accountable to another person, to God, and to yourself not to slip back into that habit, addiction, temptation, negative thought life, lustful nature, sense of inferiority, gossiping spirit, jealousy, or whatever it is you have just confessed.

As an added bonus, when you allow yourself to be vulnerable by confessing your weaknesses, you may very well be the catalyst that enables others to seek help. Your transparency may lead others to open up and draw strength from you. Best of all, by confessing our faults, we are being obedient to God. Through our confession and agreement in prayer with another, we open up a channel by which we can receive healing, strength, and deliverance. When we are set free, God's peace floods and fills our hearts, and we have pure joy.

Prayer

Dear Lord, I confess my sin of _____ to you. Please give me the strength to confess my faults to a trusted friend as well, so that we may pray together and I may gain victory over this issue in my life. I do this in obedience to your word, and I pray that you will strengthen me, heal me, and restore my joy.

There is Beauty in Correction
Day 6

"My son, despise not the chastening of the Lord;
neither be weary of his correction:
For whom the Lord loveth he correcteth;
even as a father the son in whom he delighteth"

—PROV 3:11–12 KJV

"Give instruction to a wise man, and he will be yet wiser:
teach a just man, and he will increase in learning"

—PROV 8:19 KJV

THE BOOK OF PROVERBS is filled with many scriptures reminding us that wise individuals embrace instruction, while foolish people reject correction. When we go astray, God may punish us, but his discipline is there to instruct us, to correct us, to make us wise, and to strengthen us. He corrects us, but he does not take his mercy from us (2 Sam 7:15). Sometimes it is difficult when we are in the midst of correction to understand that God's mercy still surrounds us. We fail to see that it is *because* of God's great love and mercy for us that he wants us to overcome every obstacle and quickly return to the right path.

Perhaps the closest we can come to understanding his love is when we consider the love we have for our own children. When they make mistakes we correct them, but it hurts us because we love them. We don't want to withhold any good thing from them, but we understand that through discipline they learn a valuable lesson; therefore, correction is a greater demonstration of love in the long run than leniency. Conversely, when our children humble themselves and confess their wrongdoing, our hearts melt and we embrace them with an even greater love.

This earthly parent/child relationship represents a small fraction of the love our heavenly father has for us. He longs for us to return to him with a repentant heart. When we do, he welcomes us with open arms. He restores us and forgives us. He is merciful and faithful. We cannot comprehend the depth nor the breadth of his love.

Prayer

Lord, please help me to understand that your correction in my life is there to help me grow. Help me to take those moments of correction and use them to strengthen my walk with you, knowing that you discipline me in love.

There is Beauty in Blessing
Day 7

"Surely, Lord, you bless the righteous; you surround them with your favor as with a shield"

—PS 5:12 NIV

"May the Lord bless you and protect you. May the Lord smile on you and be gracious to you. May the Lord show you his favor and give you his peace"

—NUM 6:24-26 NIV

OUR CHILDREN AND GRANDCHILDREN are precious gifts from the Lord, and they look to us for guidance and godly examples. Our children need to hear us praying for God's favor and protection over them. General prayers as they are heading off to school are great, but our children also need to hear us praying specific, meaningful blessings over their lives. Some examples of blessings we can pray over our children include praying that:

- Our children will be strong and courageous,
- They will stand for God and not fall for the tricks of the enemy.
- They will be faithful to God and to his word and surround themselves with like-minded friends (Prov. 13:20).
- They will have wisdom and be sensitive to God's voice.

- They will have discernment and know when people are genuine and when they are not.
- They will be emotionally well adjusted and have strong healthy bodies and minds.
- They will have spiritual maturity and love God with all their heart, soul, mind, and strength.
- They will keep themselves pure and holy before God.
- They will demonstrate the fruit of the spirit in their lives by showing love, compassion, humility, self-control, respect, and generosity to others (Gal 5:22–23).
- Our children will not repeat the same mistakes that we or our parents and grandparents have made (Rom 8:2).
- God will protect them and keep them all the days of their lives.

Psalm 91 and Numbers 6:24–26 offer scriptural blessings to pray over our children and other family members. Providing a strong Christian foundation and teaching them to love God and live for him is one of the most loving things we can do for our children and grandchildren. We teach them that although we can, and should, have Christians in our lives that we look up to and respect, Christ is our only perfect example (Heb 12:1–2). It is important for our children to understand that even if the strongest Christian they know fails God, that Christ will never fail them. His love is always there for us, and he is always reaching out to us with open arms to welcome us back home when we turn to him in repentance. We should also pray, now, for the husband or wife our child will one day have. Pray the same prayers over that young man or woman that you pray over your own children. You will never regret it!

When we speak these blessings over our children, we are teaching them how to pray, and God will honor our faithfulness. Hearing our prayers also helps our children understand just how much we love them and care about them. That knowledge will help them face the challenges that come their way. In short, blessing your children helps them to stand strong and points the way to Christ. (See also Matthew 18:10; Matthew 19:14.)

Prayer

Dear Heavenly Father, help me to be faithful to pray blessings and speak life over my children, grandchildren, and future generations. Help me to be bold in modeling for them how to pray and how to seek your favor and protection. Thank you, Lord, for always hearing and honoring our prayers and our obedience to your word.

There is Beauty in Restoration
Day 8

"And the cities which the Philistines had taken from Israel were restored to Israel, from Ekron even unto Gath; and the coasts thereof did Israel deliver out of the hands of the Philistines. And there was peace between Israel and the Amorites"

—1 SAM 7:14 KJV

THE GIFT OF FORGIVENESS is tremendous, and that in itself is sufficient. God cleanses us from all unrighteousness through the blood of Jesus and promises us eternal life. What more could we ask for? But God does not stop there. He restores. He restores all we have lost and more. He performs a new work in our lives. When Samuel judged Israel in 1 Samuel 7, the Philistines, who had oppressed them for years, were subdued and defeated. God heard the cries of the children of Israel. He saw their repentance, and he restored unto them all the cities the Philistines had taken from them. This passage demonstrates that God doesn't just forgive us and then leave us in the mess we are in (the mess we have created through our own sin). He mercifully and graciously restores us. He gives us more than we had before—greater joy, greater strength, greater peace, greater faith, greater wisdom and understanding, greater compassion, greater ministry, and greater love. Not because we are deserving or good, but because *he* is good and ever so faithful to fulfill all that he has promised.

Prayer

Dear Lord, please restore unto me the joy of my salvation. I confess my shortcomings and failures to you. I receive your forgiveness. Please help me to find greater joy, greater strength, and greater peace in serving you than I have ever known before. Help me to touch and bless others through the overflow of your Holy Spirit in my life.

There is Beauty in Reconciliation
Day 9

"All this is from God, who reconciled us to himself through Christ and gave us the ministry of reconciliation: that God was reconciling the world to himself in Christ, not counting people's sins against them. And he has committed to us the message of reconciliation"

—2 COR 5:18-19 (NIV)

WHAT DOES IT MEAN to be reconciled to God? We know that to be reconciled means to restore balance or harmony. When we willingly and knowingly sin, we sever our relationship with God. God does not stop loving us, but through our sin, we make ourselves an enemy of the cause of Christ (Rom 5:10). We distance ourselves from his presence and his favor. Notice that this is not something God does, it is what *we* do. We are the ones who broke our covenant with him. When we confess and turn from our sin, we are forgiven and our fellowship with God is restored.

We can compare this relationship to reconciling our checkbooks. There is a relationship between the client and the bank. As long as we keep funds in our account and do not overdraw, the relationship is harmonious. If we become careless and overdraw the account, there are consequences and the trusting relationship is damaged. When we deposit sufficient funds back into the bank, the relationship is restored. To extend this metaphor, the client has to periodically check deposits against debits to ensure that the two are in balance.

Imagine for a moment that we are the client and God is the bank. We have overdrawn our account and have no funds to deposit. We are alienated from God through our foolish choices (sin). We see the error of our ways and ask for forgiveness. Unlike the actual bank, God does not wait for us to "pay back" our overdraft. He miraculously balances our account through the applied blood of Jesus Christ. It was Christ's sacrifice on the cross that makes reconciliation possible. He paid the debt for our sin, and in calling upon his name, and trusting in his cleansing blood, we are restored to a right relationship with our heavenly father. Our sins are no longer counted against us, and he calls us his friend. He gives us favor and blesses us. Reconciliation with God, then, is to move from darkness to light, from guilt to favor, from discord to harmony, from alienation to fellowship with him. (See also Proverbs 14:9.)

Prayer

Dear Lord, thank you for the gift of reconciliation. Help me to walk close to you, stay full of your Holy Spirit, and remain in harmony with you. Help me to treasure a right relationship with you and make that my highest goal.

There is Beauty in Our Weakness and Imperfection

Day 10

"And he said unto me, My grace is sufficient for thee: for my strength is made perfect in weakness. Most gladly therefore will I rather glory in my infirmities, that the power of Christ may rest upon me"

—2 COR 12:9 KJV

"But God chose the foolish things of the world to shame the wise; God chose the weak things of the world to shame the strong. God chose the lowly things of this world and the despised things—and the things that are not—to nullify the things that are"

—1 COR 1:27-28 NIV

WHEN GOD LAYS SOMETHING on our hearts to do or opens a door of opportunity for us, we must not be afraid. Even when the thing (a new job, a business venture, new ministry, speaking engagement, giving generously, etc.) seems too big for us and beyond our abilities, God will make a way. In our weakness he is strong. In our frailty, he is glorified. It is when we need him most and rely on him, rather than on our own strength and abilities, that he shines brightest in our lives.

In the book of Deuteronomy God tells the children of Israel not to fear the nations that are dwelling in the Promised Land (7:17–26). He says if they were worried, they should remember what he did in Egypt to Pharaoh and his armies. God reminds them that he is mighty and terrible, that he is with them, and that he will deliver them from all their enemies. In other words, they do not have to trust in their own strength; God will go before them and clear a path.

When we realize how small and weak we are, we have nothing left but to trust completely in the strength of Almighty God to move on our behalf. In this way, we know for sure that it was he who made the dream come true, the vision a reality, and the crooked path straight. When we fully realize our own imperfections, we will be careful not to take glory for ourselves but to give all the glory and praise to our heavenly father. In our weakness, he is glorified. (See also Joshua 1:9.)

Prayer

Dear Lord, thank you that you never leave me. In my weakest moments you are there, and in the moment I cry out to you, you respond by giving me strength. Help me to have the courage to embrace the opportunities you send my way, and to be careful to give you all the glory.

There is Beauty in Persistence
Day 11

"Then He said to them, "Suppose one of you has a friend, and goes to him at midnight and says to him, 'Friend, lend me three loaves; for a friend of mine has come to me from a journey, and I have nothing to set before him'; and from inside he answers and says, 'Do not bother me; the door has already been shut and my children and I are in bed; I cannot get up and give you *anything*.' I tell you, even though he will not get up and give him anything because he is his friend, yet because of his persistence he will get up and give him as much as he needs"

—LUKE 11:5–8 NASB

IN THE PASSAGE ABOVE, Jesus had just been instructing the disciples how to pray, and he gave them what we now know as The Lord's Prayer as an example (Luke 11:2–4). But his instruction did not stop there. He uses a parable to teach them to be shamelessly persistent. Sometimes we think that we shouldn't bother God with our petty problems, or we think that because we have already asked once, that it demonstrates a lack of faith to ask again. But Jesus's example in Luke illustrates that our persistence touches him. He wants us to seek him with tenacity—to pursue him, to keep making our petitions known. Our shameless persistence touches him. It is not wrong or weak to ask again and again until we receive what we are in need of. Then in verse 9 of Luke 11, Jesus goes on to say, "So I say to you, ask, and it will be given to you; seek, and you will find; knock, and it will be opened to you" (NASB). We are his children, and he enjoys blessing us with good gifts.

When I was eight years old, my sister Mary and I wanted a bike for Christmas. We had never had our own bike before, and our family had very little money to provide such a luxury item. Naturally, the first time we asked our parents, we were met with a resounding, "No." Over the months and weeks leading up to Christmas, we continued to ask and reason with them. When the usual negative responses did not deter us, our parents began to give our request more serious thought. We were willing to share a bike, and we told them that bike was the only gift we wanted that year. My parents came to realize how much owning a bicycle meant to us, and they found a way to make it happen. That Christmas, there was a beautiful blue bike under the tree with our names on it. Once again I point to Matthew 7:11. We are God's children, and he loves to bless us with good gifts, but sometimes, he wants to see that passion, that fire, and some evidence that the thing we are petitioning him for is truly important to us, not just a passing whim. He honors our shameless persistence. (See also Philippians 4: 6–8.)

Prayer

Dear Lord, thank you for teaching us how to pray. Please help me to seek the things that you desire for my life. Help me to pursue you and to be persistent in bringing my petitions before you. Thank you for your goodness and your faithfulness.

There is Beauty in Obedience
Day 12

"But Samuel replied: 'Does the Lord delight in burnt offerings and sacrifices as much as in obeying the Lord? To obey is better than sacrifice, and to heed is better than the fat of rams'"

—1 SAM 15:22 NIV

"Hear, Israel, the decrees and laws I declare in your hearing today. Learn them and be sure to follow them"

—DEUT 5:1 NIV

WE SEE IN DEUTERONOMY that God rescued Israel out of slavery and made a covenant with them. He promised to bring them to the Promised Land, but he had some expectations of them as well. Moses shares the Ten Commandments that God gave him for the people and instructs them to obey those ordinances and to stay away from idols and false gods (Deut 5:7–21 NIV). In verse 9, God tells them, "You shall not worship them or serve them; for I, the Lord your God, am a jealous God." Although, this scripture was written long ago to the children of Israel, it has practical application today. God desires to be first in our lives. He wants us to follow after him with our whole heart. When we make room in our lives for the things that are not of God, and give them prominence over our time with the Lord and over his commandments, we are building false idols. God is still a jealous God, and there are consequences for our rebellion.

Verse 9 continues by stating that God will "[punish] the children for the sin of the parents to the third and the fourth generations of those who hate [him]." That is a difficult message to receive, but, fortunately, there is also good news. If we love God and obey his commandments, he says in verse 10 he will show his unfailing love to "a thousand generations of those who love [him] and keep [his] commandments." What a marvelous legacy to leave to our children! God longs to bless us, but we must first turn away from our sin and follow after him with all our heart, soul, mind, and strength. Second, we need to ask God to lift the curse of sin that may have been passed down through the sin of our parents and grandparents. Third, we need to pray a covering over our children and grandchildren that they will not suffer for our sins and the sins of our ancestors. Finally, we need to teach our children to obey God and to worship him only. When we are obedient, God promises to lavish unfailing love on us and our children for many generations to come. What better way to protect our children and ensure the blessings of God in their lives?

(For a complete context of this entry, read Deuteronomy 5:1–22.)

Prayer

Lord, please help me to obey your commands and keep you first in my life. I pray that you will break the bondage of sin from my life and from the lives of my children. Help me to be a strong leader for my children and grandchildren, and I ask for your blessings and favor upon them.

There is Beauty in Fellowship
Day 13

"Come near to God and he will come near to you"

—JAS 4:8 NIV

"But seek ye first the kingdom of God, and his righteousness; and all these things shall be added unto you"

—MATT 6:33 KJV

SPENDING TIME WITH GOD in prayer and in daily Bible reading is one of the most important things, if not the most important thing, we can do to strengthen our spiritual walk. Many times we become so weighed down with the stress and demands of our daily lives that we push time with God far down on the list of our priorities. The truth is, in order to stay strong and have the tools we need to cope with the cares of this world, we must make time alone with him a priority. We cannot afford not to.

Matthew 6:21 states, "For where your treasure is, there will your heart be also" (KJV). How we prioritize our time says quite a bit about where our treasure is. Even if it means getting out of bed 20—30 minutes earlier, we must make time to put God first in our lives. When we spend time with him, his presence is with us throughout the day, and that changes everything. And working for God is not a substitute for praying or Bible reading. It is often tempting to become so consumed with working for the church or a particular ministry or charitable organization that we forget to nurture own relationship with God. By all means, as Christians, we should serve others, but if we are allowing those activities to absorb so much of our time that we no longer have time to spend with our heavenly father, then we are allowing that activity to rob us of our spiritual walk and ultimately our joy. This kind of over commitment can be very stressful and allows the enemy to gain a foothold in our lives. When approached with new opportunities to serve, we should pray over each assignment, and make sure it is what God is leading us to do. Ask yourself whether or not doing that task will bring you closer to him. You can even ask for a trial period, say one month, or make a limited commitment for three months. After that time has elapsed, you can pray about whether to recommit and assess how that activity is impacting your own spiritual walk.

God is faithful, and he loves a willing heart. He will show us where he wants us, but we must make certain that our own spirit is being fed. When we are full of the Holy Spirit, we overflow with joy and are able to minister to others through our abundance. (See also Proverbs 3:5–6.)

Prayer

Dear Lord, thank you for providing your word as a daily guide for my life. Help me to make fellowship with you a priority each and every day. I need your Holy Spirit dwelling in me and working through me in all that I do. Thank you, Lord, for your faithfulness.

There is Beauty in Trust: Overcoming Guilt (Part 1)

Day 14

> "There is therefore now no condemnation to them which are in Christ Jesus, who walk not after the flesh, but after the Spirit"
>
> —ROM 8:1 KJV

> "I, even I, am he who blots out your transgressions, for my own sake, and remembers your sins no more"
>
> —ISA 43:25 NIV

ONCE WE HAVE CONFESSED our sins and accepted God's forgiveness in our lives, we must realize that we are free from condemnation. We must trust that his promises are true. One of the cruelest tricks of the enemy—the accuser of the brethren—is to remind us of our past sins, our failures, and our shortcomings (Rev 12:10). He tries to make us feel that we are not worthy to praise God, to approach God's throne in prayer, to ask for healing, or to ask for any help at all. The enemy tries to make us feel that we are not good enough. We must remember that it is not because of our goodness that we can approach God's throne, but it is because of *his* great goodness and compassion for us. He makes us worthy through the blood of Jesus Christ. The scriptures tell us that "where sin abounded, grace did much more abound" (Rom 5:20 KJV). God's grace is sufficient for all our sins. We know that in our hearts, yet the enemy wants us to think we are not forgiven. He will bring up past sin to create feelings of guilt and shame. These feelings distract us from God and hinder our praise to him. In fact, the enemy is the only one who remembers our sins against us at all. God has buried them in the depths of the sea. For his word says: "You will again have compassion on us; you will tread our sins underfoot and hurl all our iniquities into the depths of the sea" (Mic 7:9 NIV). They are gone and forgotten. If we have accepted the cleansing blood of Jesus Christ we are purified and clean before him and made worthy to approach his throne. Therefore, the trick of the enemy is clear; he wants to keep us focused on ourselves rather than focused on what God has done for us, but it is when we remember God's grace and great love for us, and lavish our praise and adoration on him, that we are truly blessed.

Prayer

Dear Lord, I accept your forgiveness in my life. I believe that you have buried my sins in the depths of the sea. I thank you for making me worthy to approach your throne and offer my praises to you. When I am reminded of my past, help me to remember the sacrifice you made for me, and turn those thoughts into praise to you!

There is Beauty in Praise: Overcoming Guilt (Part 2)

Day 15

"For the Lord your God is the one who goes with you to fight for you against your enemies to give you victory"

—DEUT 20:4 NIV

"But thou art holy, O thou that inhabitest the praises of Israel"

—PSALM 22:3 KJV

I HAVE OFTEN HEARD preachers say, "When the enemy reminds you of your past, remind him of his future." As followers of Christ, we must keep in mind who wins this war. The scriptures tell us that "we are more than conquerors through him who loved us" (Rom 8:37 KJV). We are victorious through the blood of the Lamb! Hebrews 4:16 states, "Let us therefore come boldly unto the throne of grace, that we may obtain mercy, and find grace to help in time of need" (KJV). Accepting God's grace in our lives sets us free from guilt and condemnation. Every time the enemy tries to bring feelings of guilt upon us, we need to turn that thought, that attack, into a praise to God Almighty! Praising God invites God's presence. Praise him and thank him for his grace. Praise for his strength and power. Praise him for his majesty and his awesome goodness. Thank him for his cleansing blood—the blood of Jesus. The enemy will not stick around when we praise our heavenly father. Our praises to God drive out the negative thoughts and lead us forward in victory.

Prayer

Dear Lord, help me to turn every negative thought into a praise to you. Help me to praise you even in the darkest times and to remember that I am victorious through you.

Finding Joy:
Forgive Others Unconditionally

Day 16

"Bear with each other and forgive one another if any of you has a grievance against someone. Forgive as the Lord forgave you"

—COL 3:13 NIV

ONE MAJOR OBSTACLE TO experiencing joy in our lives is pain. I am speaking of emotional pain—pain caused by words, by offenses against us, by neglect, by betrayal, and by abuse. Some people live with physical abuse, sexual abuse, verbal abuse, emotional abuse, and it leaves deep scars. This deep-seated pain will hinder our walk with God if we allow them to. Pain can cripple and impair us spiritually just as physical pain can have a crippling effect on our bodies. Emotional pain can prevent us from experiencing the abundant joy God has for us. We need to be set free.

The first step in being set free from that pain is forgiveness. It is human nature to want to hold onto offenses; we often harbor bitterness and resentment, and even hate, for the person who caused us pain. In doing so, we nurture those memories and keep them alive. In effect, we irritate the wound and keep it from healing. The Lord's Prayer, found in Matthew 6:9–13, states: "And forgive us our debts, as we have forgiven our debtors." Verse 14 of that same chapter makes clear the importance of forgiveness: "For if ye forgive men their trespasses, your heavenly Father will also forgive you" (KJV). Verse 15 then delivers a very sobering message: "But if ye forgive not men their trespasses, neither will your Father forgive your trespasses." This passage demonstrates that for the Christian, forgiveness if not optional. If we want our heavenly father's forgiveness, we must be willing to forgive others.

Holding onto the pain of past offenses does not hurt the wrongdoer; it only hurts the victim. Harboring unforgiveness keeps us bound and keeps us from entering into the fullness of God's joy. When we release those offenses, when we give them to God and truly forgive the perpetrator, God sets us free. There is a beautiful reciprocity in forgiveness. As long as we hold onto hate and resentment, we are bound. As soon as we forgive, God forgives our trespasses and takes us to a new level of joy in him.

Once we have forgiven, we need to get rid of reminders. Throw out photos, notes, journals, emails, and similar items that remind us of the hurt. First Corinthians 13:4 teaches us that love "keeps no record of wrongs" (NIV). Truly release those memories to God and allow his Holy Spirit to bring peace and joy to our hearts. When we are set free from pain, we are free to praise him and walk in joy. We bless others from the abundance of our overflow. One word of caution, forgiving others does not mean that we can forget what happened. Only God can do that. When the enemy tries to bring up those painful memories, turn that thought into a praise to God. "Resist the enemy and he will flee from you" (Jas 4:7 KJV). Glorify God and thank him for the ability he has given you to forgive. Thank him for the peace and joy he has brought into your life.

Prayer

Dear Lord, you see my pain. Please help me to release that pain to you. By faith, I forgive all those who have hurt me and contributed to the pain in my life. I call each one by name, and I speak forgiveness to that person. I forgive _____ for _____. I release that offense to you in Jesus's name. Thank you, Lord, for your forgiveness in my life.

Finding Joy: Forgive Yourself
Day 17

"If we confess our sins, he is faithful and just to forgive us our sins, and to cleanse us from all unrighteousness"

—1 JOHN 1:9 KJV

"There is therefore now no condemnation to them which are in Christ Jesus, who walk not after the flesh, but after the Spirit"

—ROM 8:1 KJV

"He hath not dealt with us after our sins; nor rewarded us according to our iniquities. For as the heaven is high above the earth, so great is his mercy toward them that fear him"

—PS 103:10–11 KJV

Although forgiving those who have injured us can be a challenge, forgiving ourselves is often the most difficult task of all. We tend to be harder on ourselves than we are on anyone else. We think, "If you only knew my story, you would not think I deserved forgiveness." Yet when we see another person in the same (or similar) situation, we are moved with compassion and open our hearts to them. Why do we find it so hard to forgive ourselves?

Romans 3:23 states: For all have sinned and come short of the glory of God." To God, sin is sin. One sin is not worse than another; we all need God's mercy and forgiveness. We need to stop getting caught up in how "bad" our sin is and realize that it is not about us. It is about God and his abundant grace and mercy. He died so that we "might have life and have it more abundantly" (John 10:10 KJV). When we pick up that mantle of guilt and defeat and wear it around like a shroud, we are doubting Christ's ability to truly forgive. The apostle Paul writes, "For we walk by faith and not by sight" (2 Cor 5:7 KJV). Walking by faith means trusting God. If we have faith, it follows that there will be an absence of fear and doubt. Faith is the opposite of fear. We are not to focus on what we see, but on what God's word says. God's word says that if we confess our sins to him, he is faithful and just to forgive us. (See 1 John 1:9 above.) Does that mean we are ineffective as Christians if we feel guilt or doubt? Absolutely not! We just need to turn to the scriptures and remind ourselves (and our enemy—the deceiver) what God's word says about us.

One of the best scriptures to quote when doubt tries to creep in is Romans 8:1: "There is therefore now no condemnation to them which are in Christ Jesus, who walk not after the flesh, but after the Spirit" (KJV). No matter what we have done, what pain we have inflicted on others (or even on ourselves), we need to realize that the blood of Jesus covers that sin. We need to confess that sin and turn away from it, and then accept Christ's cleansing blood that purifies us. When God looks at us, he does not see our dirty, sinful nature; he sees us clothed in robes of righteousness— the righteousness of Christ Jesus. Second Corinthians 5:21 states: For he hath made him to be sin for us, who knew no sin; that we might be made the righteousness of God in him (KJV). This is the way we need to begin to see ourselves, clothed in the righteousness of Christ. When we can accept God's complete forgiveness in our lives, we can forgive ourselves and walk in victory. We can truly experience *the joy of our salvation* (Ps 51:12 KJV). It is when we are walking in joy and victory that we can touch others and use our own experiences to help them overcome as well. (See also 2 Corinthians 5:17 and Philippians 3:13–14.)

Prayer

Dear Lord, thank you for your forgiveness. Help me to accept the mercy and grace you have extended to me, and please help me to forgive myself. Help me to see myself clothed in your righteousness and made worthy by the blood of the Lamb. I ask you to restore my joy and help me to use my experiences to minister to others.

Finding Joy: Embrace Healing

Day 18

> "The Lord is close to the brokenhearted
> and saves those who are crushed in spirit"
>
> —PS 34:18 NIV

ONCE WE HAVE GIVEN all of our pain to the Lord, accepted his forgiveness, and forgiven ourselves, we are ready to embrace healing and live the life he planned for us all along. Does that mean that we just pretend that our past never happened? Absolutely not. Our friends, our family, and especially, our children, need to see an individual that was broken but has been healed and is living victoriously. We can be forthright and real with our children. We can allow them to see that although we made mistakes, we have overcome and are living in obedience to God's word. We are not giving them a license to sin; we are demonstrating to them our humanity and providing a living example of the grace, mercy, and love of our heavenly Father who never let us go.

God has abundant life planned for us. There are hurting people he wants us to minister to. There are people in the situation we were in who need to see that there is forgiveness when we come to him with a broken heart, and that God's love is still there for us. He never leaves us. The pain, guilt, and fear were simply distractions, noise, that kept us from hearing God's voice. Now we are ready to dig deep into his word, spend time in prayer for others, and listen to what God is speaking to our hearts. He will give us divine appointments with people who will need to hear our testimony. Each time we share our faith with others we become stronger. It doesn't matter whether we are planting seeds, nurturing a seed planted by another, or reaping the harvest, God will bless us and increase our joy when we minister to others. (See 1 Corinthians 3:4–9.) God has instilled gifts in each of us that he wants to use for his glory. Romans 11:36 states, "For from him and through him and for him are all things. To him be the glory forever! Amen" (NIV). When we truly embrace our healing, we can allow God's spirit to flow through us and reignite the passion and gifts he has given us. If that gift is singing, sing for his glory. If that gift is communication, use your words to bring healing, comfort, and joy. If that gift is playing an instrument, do it for the glory of God. If your gift is writing, use your writing to uplift. If your gift is administration, use that talent for God. If your gift is art, create work that brings glory to God Almighty. In doing so, you will bless others, and you also will be blessed. All God requires from us is a willing heart, and he will provide the path for us to minister.

Prayer

Dear Lord, help me to embrace the healing you have provided for my spirit and my emotions. I give it all to you. Help me to use the talents and gifts you have given me to bless others for your glory.

Finding Joy: Think Positively

Day 19

"Nehemiah said, 'Go and enjoy choice food and sweet drinks, and send some to those who have nothing prepared. This day is holy to our Lord. Do not grieve, for the joy of the Lord is your strength'"

—NEH 8:10 NIV

"The joy of the Lord is your strength." This little phrase holds the key to living a victorious life. When we are full of the joy of the Lord, the joy that comes from knowing him and walking close to him, we are strong. Joy gives us strength to stand, to witness, to minister, to give, to teach, to exhort, and to reach others. Joy makes us invulnerable to attacks from the enemy. When we are full of God's Holy Spirit, we minister to others through the overflow of his joy in our lives. "But the fruit of the spirit is love, joy, peace, longsuffering, gentleness, goodness, faith, meekness, temperance: against such there is no law"(Gal 5:22 KJV). Our adversary, understands the key to our strength and has many tricks to try to steal our joy and to weaken our spiritual walk. John 10:10 states, "The thief cometh not, but for to steal, and to kill, and to destroy: I am come that they might have life, and that they might have it more abundantly." That enemy will bring many distractions into our lives to try to rob us of our joy. Some of the tools he uses have already been mentioned: pain, guilt, fear, stress, worry, and, of course, sin. When we nurture these things in our lives and begin to dwell on them, they hinder the flow of the Holy Spirit. They kill our joy. They weaken and debilitate us. They prevent and distract us from the work God has called us to do. We must learn to cast those negative thoughts aside and focus on God's goodness. Right attitudes begin with right thoughts. As we begin to focus on the blessings God has so generously provided, our love and appreciation for him grows, and our joy increases. "Finally, brethren, whatsoever things are true, whatsoever things are honest, whatsoever things are just, whatsoever things are pure, whatsoever things are lovely, whatsoever things are of good report; if there be any virtue, and if there be any praise, think on these things" (Phil 4:8 KJV).

Prayer

Dear Lord, please help me focus on the blessings in my life. Please cleanse my mind of negativity, and teach me to meditate on truth and to listen to reports that are honest and just. Help me to turn every negative thought into a praise to you.

Finding Joy: Renew Daily

Day 20

"Create in me a clean heart, O God;
and renew a right spirit within me"

—PS 51:10 KJV

ONE OF THE GREATEST obstacles in our lives that can rob us of true joy is our thought life. Sinful acts begin as sinful thoughts. The enemy uses those secret places in our hearts and minds to undermine the work God wants to do. He plants thoughts and ideas that we don't even want to be there! When we come before the Lord, we must come with clean hands and a pure heart. How can we, with our frail, human nature, achieve that? We must confess all of our sins (even the secret ones we try to hold onto) daily: the impure thoughts, strife, jealousy, envy, the show we watched that did not bring glory to God, the gossip we shared, the images we viewed that took us further away from God's plan for us, and ask God to fill us with his precious Holy Spirit. We cannot attain perfection on our own, but through the sacrifice of Jesus Christ and his Holy Spirit working in us, we can stand clean before him. But it does require a daily walk with him. The longer we go without confessing our sins and praying for strength, the more distant that ideal will start to seem. It becomes easier and easier to slip into a lifestyle that we know is not pleasing to God and does not bring us joy.

One of my favorite verses to quote daily is Psalm 19:14: "Let the words of my mouth, and the meditation of my heart, be acceptable in thy sight, O Lord, my strength, and my redeemer (KJV). The psalmist knew that peace and joy begin in the heart and in the mind. If an individual finds it difficult to control his/her tongue, that person has not yet mastered his/her mind. We must daily bring our thoughts under subjection to the Holy Spirit and our actions will follow. When we dwell on the things of God, our greatest desire is to please him. We have often heard it said, "What goes in is what comes out." That is so true in the spiritual realm. If we are feeding our minds with ungodly music, spiteful gossip, trashy television shows, racy novels and movies, and yes, the latest news feed on social media, we will likely find it very difficult to then behave in a Christ-like manner when a challenging situation arises. Even on our best days, we need to be full of the Holy Spirit in order to remain victorious in the day-to-day challenges that come our way. (See also, Ephesians 4: 23–24 and 1 John 5: 21.)

Prayer

Dear Lord, please help me to renew my heart and mind daily. Reveal to me anything that is not pleasing to you, and help me to confess that weakness to you. Help me to fill my heart and soul with things that are pleasing to you and bring honor and glory to your name. Please let my thoughts, words, and actions always be acceptable in your sight.

Finding Joy: Practice Discretion
Day 21

> "If any man among you seem to be religious, and bridleth not his tongue, but deceiveth his own heart, this man's religion is vain"
>
> —JAS 1:26 KJV

THE WORD OF GOD instructs us to keep a tight rein on our tongue, yet this is one of the hardest things to do. In fact, we cannot do it alone; we need the power of the Holy Spirit working in us and through us. James 3:8 says, "But the tongue can no man tame; it is an unruly evil, full of deadly poison" (KJV). So how can anyone control his or her tongue? As hard as we try, and as good as our intentions may be, it is extremely difficult to hold our tongue in certain situations. There are two essential elements we must realize:

1. We cannot do it alone; we need the power of the Holy Spirit.
2. It is a process, not an overnight success.

The process is described in Chapter 3 of the book of James. Just as a horse does not adapt immediately to the bridle or the reins, the tongue has to be gently and patiently coaxed and trained into submission. We start our training by meditating on God's word. (See also Psalm 19:14.) There is quite a bit of truth in that. If we are in God's word daily, letting it speak to us, we are less likely to speak in anger or contempt, to gossip, to slander, to tell tasteless jokes, or tear down someone else. Instead, our words will bring life and light to others. We will have compassion and build up others. We must also be filled with the Holy Spirit of God. We need his spirit to purge us and cleanse us of everything that is not of him.

We need a daily renewing of our minds. When we are full of God's spirit, he will prompt us and give us words to speak. He will also put a check on our spirit when we are about to say the wrong thing. That check, that little tug we feel inside, that hesitation, teaches us to stay quiet—to hold back hurtful words and thoughts. As we train our tongues, we become more adept at it and much stronger. Again, it does not happen overnight, but we can improve daily, taking on small challenges at first. Pretty soon practicing discretion becomes a habit. If we stumble, we learn not to beat ourselves up, but to get back up and keep going—keep growing. Learning to control our tongues frees us from the guilt of wrongdoing, and increases our joy. (See also James 3:2–10, Proverbs 12:18, and Proverbs 16:20.)

Prayer

Dear Lord, I confess my weakness to you. I need the power of your Holy Spirit to help me control my tongue. Please purge and cleanse me from everything that is not of you. Help me to meditate on your word and to respond in love to those around me.

Finding Joy:
Meditate on God's Word (Part 1)

Day 22

"Keep this Book of the Law always on your lips; meditate on it day and night, so that you may be careful to do everything written in it. Then you will be prosperous and successful"

—JOSH 1:8 NIV

"Thy word have I hid in mine heart, that I might not sin against thee"

—PS 119:11 KJV

GOD WANTS US TO study the instruction book he has given us, his word. Jesus is the Word of God made flesh (John 1:14). When Jesus walked on Earth, man had the very word of God living and dwelling among them. When Jesus ascended to heaven, God sent the Holy Spirit to be our comforter and guide, but he also provided us his written word. People often say, "How do I know when God is speaking to me? How can I hear his voice?" His word, the Bible, is his voice to his children. When we read the word he has given us, he quickens it and makes it alive for us. Hebrews 4:12 teaches, "For the word of God is quick, and powerful, and sharper than any two-edged sword, piercing even to the dividing asunder of soul and spirit, and of the joints and marrow, and is a discerner of the thoughts and intents of the heart" (KJV). The Bible is not a collector's item to be left on the shelf and gather dust. It is a link to the very heart and mind of God. He wants us to think about it, to consider it, to ponder it, to know it, and to hide it deep within our hearts (Ps 119:11).

When we are faithful to meditate on the word of God, our spiritual walk and our moral character are strengthened. We see in the opening verse (above) that blessing follows obedience. When we meditate on God's word, he blesses us by giving us strength to stand against temptation, and he provides us with a defense against all the weapons of the enemy, such as fear, doubt, condemnation, guilt, stress, and worry. In addition, God's word tells us that when we obey him, we will succeed and prosper. Right living and a clear conscience lead to a healthier, more prosperous, and fulfilling life: financially, emotionally, spiritually and physically. God's word provides principles for daily living that have stood the test of time. As an added bonus, when we know we are doing our utmost to please the Lord, we are filled with peace and joy. From this abundance, we are able to pursue the work God has called us to, which is to be a light to a lost and dying world. (See also Proverbs 3:6–8 and Proverbs 4:20–22.)

Prayer

Dear Lord, help me to hide your word deep within my heart that I might not sin against you. Help me to meditate on your word and to obey the instructions you have given us here on earth. Thank you for the strength, joy, and peace that come with faithfulness to you.

Finding Joy: Meditate on God's Word (Part 2)

Day 23

> "Keep this Book of the Law always on your lips; meditate on it day and night, so that you may be careful to do everything written in it. Then you will be prosperous and successful
>
> —JOSH 1:8 NIV

> "Fix these words of mine in your hearts and minds; tie them as symbols on your hands and bind them on your foreheads. Teach them to your children, talking about them when you sit at home and when you walk along the road, when you lie down and when you get up. Write them on the doorframes of your houses and on your gates, so that your days and the days of your children may be many in the land the Lord swore to give your ancestors, as many as the days that the heavens are above the earth"
>
> —DEUT. 11:18-21 NIV

THE FOOD WE EAT and beverages we consume provide the energy and fortification our physical bodies need to live each day. If we fail to eat and drink, we soon become weak and faint and have no strength to cope with simple tasks. Similarly, what we feed our spirit is what we have to live on and face the spiritual challenges each day brings. If we feed our spirit rubbish, then we have no strength to stand when problems arise, and we suffer setbacks or even failure. When we dwell on God's word, meditate on him, and obey his commands, we are strengthened. We have the sustenance and strength we need to withstand every attack of the enemy.

Satan has tried to corrupt every gift that God has given us from language and music to art and dance. What God intended to uplift and provide joy, Satan has used to inject sin and corruption into the hearts and minds of people. The same goes for literature. God gave us the ability to read and communicate, and he provided his word, the Bible, as a resource to remind us of his commands and his great love for us. It is the only book we need! It is certainly not wrong to read other books or listen to music, but when we allow those things to crowd out and replace our time with God and his word, we have fallen victim to one of the enemy's most successful traps. If the enemy can pull us away from God's word, he can weaken our spiritual stand. This is why God commanded Joshua and the children of Israel to study the word of God, to meditate on it day and night. He gave the children of Israel, and us, all the tools we need to stand strong and live victoriously. It just requires discipline and faithfulness on our part. When we make time with God a priority, we soon find that the benefits far outweigh any perceived sacrifices. In fact, we come to treasure and protect that time with the Lord and look forward to it as something precious, because that is exactly what it is!

Prayer

Dear Lord, help me not to let the things of the world crowd out your voice. Help me to make spending time in your word and focusing on you a priority. Let my music, the books I read, the time I spend on the Internet, my conversations, my hobbies, and my gifts and talents bring honor and glory to you.

Finding Joy: Let Go of Injustice
Day 24

> "The very fact that you have lawsuits among you means you have been completely defeated already. Why not rather be wronged? Why not rather be cheated?"
>
> —1 COR 6:7 NIV

ONE OF THE HARDEST things to do is to let go of injustice. I have always been very fairness and justice oriented. When I see injustice, it angers me. When I am the victim of injustice (or I have caused an injustice), I feel unsettled, and I want to talk it over with the other individual to try to clear the air (Matt 5:23). There is nothing wrong with confronting problems, as long as we can keep a Christ-like spirit; we are certainly not to slander that person to others.

Recently I came across a scripture I had read before, but it hit me in a whole new way. It caused me to rethink my response to injustice. Someone close to me recently accused me of something that simply was not true, and it hurt. I have made plenty of mistakes, and I like to think that I am quick to take ownership of them, but this person was assigning thoughts and motives, and even words, to me that were completely false. I was praying about whether or not I should talk it over with this individual. Then I went to my daily Bible reading, and I just happened to be reading in 1 Corinthians, Chapter 6. Paul is rebuking the Corinthians for suing each other, their brothers and sisters in the church, and taking their cases to the secular courts. In verse 7 he says, "The very fact that you have lawsuits among you means you have been completely defeated already. Why not rather be wronged? Why not rather be cheated?" (NIV). That scripture grabbed my attention. Even though my situation does not involve a lawsuit, it does involve a disagreement between two believers. For Christians to even have such a dispute represents a failure, a weakness. To be able to rise above the injustice, forgive, and let it go demonstrates much more spiritual maturity than making sure both sides are heard. Naturally, there are some injustices that are so serious that they need to be dealt with through legal channels or by some other means, but petty disputes have no place in the Kingdom of God. (See also Matthew 5:44.)

Prayer

Lord, please help me to love those and pray for those who treat me unjustly. Help me to remember that you, too, were falsely accused, and you bore it without defending yourself. I recognize my weakness in wanting to seek justice, but I trust you, and I know that there is blessing in being obedient to your word.

Finding Joy: Seek Diligently
Day 25

"Seek the Lord and His strength. Seek His face continually"

—1 CHR 16:11 NASB

God's word says "seek and ye shall find" (Matt 7:7). God does not set us up to do the impossible, so that means that when we search for him, we *can* find him. "And ye shall seek me, and find me, when ye shall search for me with all your heart" (Jer 29:13 KJV). So, how do we seek him? We are seeking him when we read his word; we are seeking to hear from him. When we pray, we are seeking to commune with him through the power of the Holy Spirit that works and lives in us. Through giving we seek to honor him with our finances and our time; therefore, praying, reading God's word, and giving are all ways we seek to draw closer to him.

In Matthew, Jesus teaches that when we give to others, we are, in essence, giving to him. "The King will reply, 'Truly I tell you, whatever you did for one of the least of these brothers and sisters of mine, you did for me'" (Matt 25:40 NIV). Also, in giving, we demonstrate gratitude for all he does for us and acknowledge that we can never repay that debt. We give because we are humbled by his overwhelming, unfailing love for us, and we seek to demonstrate that love to someone else—someone in need. In giving to that individual or group, we experience Christ's love in our hearts. We receive (in joy, contentment, peace with our Lord) far more than the time, talent, or money that we give. But the *act* of giving in the right spirit allows us to encounter God and feel his presence with us. It is another way to seek him. If we could always stay in that spirit of giving, we would move one step closer to living in communion with him.

Prayer

Dear Lord, I run to you. I seek after you with my whole heart. Please do not take your Holy Spirit from me. Please help me to walk in your spirit and live a life pleasing to you.

Finding Joy: Spread the Light
Day 26

"For you were once darkness, but now you are light in the Lord. Live as children of light (for the fruit of the light consists in all goodness, righteousness and truth"

—EPH 5:8–9 NIV

AVOIDING GOSSIP AND SLANDER is one thing, but using our tongue as an instrument of peace is another. We are to be light in the darkness, demonstrating love to all those around us. People are attracted to the light. When the light of God's love shines through us, people are drawn to us as well. The world is looking for something real, something authentic. That doesn't mean perfection. We can be honest about where we are with God and where we've been, but people need to see Christ's love in us. We are to walk in love, giving ourselves to others and not thinking about what we can gain from the interaction. This is sacrificial giving and a true demonstration of love.

One way we shine the light of God is through our words. Our words need to be life-giving. They need to bring comfort, peace, security, and assurance. Speaking a kind word to the cashier at the grocery store, praising a co-worker for a great idea, showing appreciation for the hard work of a custodian, expressing appreciation to family members, complimenting a friend (or a stranger) are all ways we can spread light. And this doesn't mean just the people we like; it includes the people who are difficult to love. We all have those people in our lives, and they may test the limits of our spiritual walk. Matthew 5:43–44 says, "Ye have heard that it hath been said, Thou shalt love thy neighbour, and hate thine enemy. But I say unto you, love your enemies, bless them that curse you, do good to them that hate you, and pray for them which despitefully use you, and persecute you" (KJV).

The people who behave the worst may be the ones who are hurting the most. Praising, exhorting, thanking, congratulating, and comforting are all words the world needs to hear, and those life-giving words open the door for more communication. People begin to see us as a positive force in their lives and may even seek us out when they need prayer or guidance. Forgetting about our own needs and speaking kindly to others is a practical demonstration of God's love. When we minister to the needs of others, Christ will in turn send others (at the appropriate time) to minister to us. (See also Proverbs 16:24.)

Prayer

Dear Lord, I thank you for the love you extend to me daily. I am ready to be a source of comfort and encouragement to others. Please let my words bring light and life to those around me.

Finding Joy: Judge Not

Day 27

"And the great dragon was cast out, that old serpent, called the devil, and Satan, which deceiveth the whole world: he was cast out into the earth, and his angels were cast out with him. And I heard a loud voice saying in heaven, Now is come salvation, and strength, and the kingdom of our God, and the power of his Christ: for the accuser of our brethren is cast down, which accused them before our God day and night"

—REV 12:9-12 KJV

HAVE YOU EVER PURPOSED in your heart to speak well of others and to show God's love only to fail as soon as an opportunity presents itself? Well, you are not alone. The apostle Paul knew what it was to wrestle with the flesh. In Romans 7:21–23 he writes, "So I find this law at work: Although I want to do good, evil is right there with me. For in my inner being I delight in God's law; but I see another law at work in me, waging war against the law of my mind and making me a prisoner of the law of sin at work within me" (NIV). I believe we can all relate to this struggle against the flesh. I have often left for work with a strong resolve to speak well of those around me, yet time and time again, I find myself judging people's motives or getting caught up in gossip or criticism. Then I feel guilty and have to repent. This can become a vicious cycle in our lives, but God wants to break that cycle.

Right words, affirming words, begin with right thoughts. I have said this before, but it bears repeating: words and actions follow from what we *think*. Every word we speak has a foundation in our thought life. When we assign pure motives to another individual, our words about that person will be much more charitable. When we pray blessings over an individual, we will be much less apt to criticize him or her. That doesn't mean we ignore sin or disrespectful behavior; we just have to realize that God is their judge. God wants us to be more concerned with our own heart than the actions of others. When judgmental thoughts come into our mind about someone, we need to capture that thought and get rid of it. Second Corinthians 10:5 instructs us to "[cast] down imaginations, and every high thing that exalteth itself against the knowledge of God, and [bring] into captivity every thought to the obedience of Christ" (KJV). If we are struggling with a particular person, we need to replace uncharitable thoughts with affirming thoughts and genuinely pray for that person. By letting ourselves empathize and feel compassion for people in our thought life, we set ourselves up to speak well of them when the time comes. When we criticize others, we act as an accuser against them, which is the role of our adversary (see the opening scripture). As Christians, we do not want to put ourselves in that position. How much more faithful and fulfilling to submit to the Holy Spirit of God and to show love and compassion to others in thought, word, and deed. By doing so, we strengthen the fruit of the Spirit in our lives (Gal 5:22–23) which in turn increases our joy. The rewards of speaking kindly are so much more lasting and satisfying than the guilt and emptiness of judgment and criticism. (See also Proverbs 16:28.)

Prayer

Dear Lord, thank you for your forgiveness and faithfulness in my life. Please help me to think and speak kindly of those around me. Help me not to judge but to pray for others and empathize with what they may be feeling. Help me to gain victory over that impulse to think the worst, and instead, to be your hand extended to all people. Help me to bring light and life to a dying world.

Finding Joy: Claim God's Promises
Day 28

"See, I have placed the land before you; go in and possess the land which the Lord swore to give to your fathers, to Abraham, to Isaac, and to Jacob, to them and their descendants after them"

—DEUT 1:8 NASB

GOD WANTS US TO take bold steps of faith and take possession of the blessings he has promised us. God told the children of Israel in verse 8 (above) that he was giving them all the land of Canaan, but they were fearful because the land was already inhabited. God was essentially saying, "It's yours; all you have to do is go in and take it!" It already belonged to them, but it did require a step of faith on their part. Then in verses 29 of Deuteronomy 1, God tells them not to dread and not to be afraid, that he will go before them and fight for them. And I love verse 31 that reminds them, "you saw how the Lord your God carried you just as a man carries his son" throughout the wilderness and into the land of promise (Deuteronomy 1:31, NASB). Once again, we see the unfailing love of our heavenly father. Even though the Israelites had failed him repeatedly and fallen into idol worship, he forgave them and welcomed them home. He promised to be with them, to go before them and fight for them, and to fulfill his promise to them.

The Lord loves us with that same unfailing love. We are his children, too! Every believer has dreams and aspirations. They have stirrings in their spirit of things the Lord wants them to accomplish, whether it's sharing their faith, running for public office, heading up projects at work, starting a Bible study group, or something similar. God loves us and wants to bless us with good gifts. Matthew 7:11 (NIV) states, "If ye then, being evil, know how to give good gifts unto your children, how much more shall your Father which is in heaven give good things to them that ask him?" The land, (whatever God has promised us) is ours, but we have to be willing to go in and possess it. When we prayerfully seek him and take that first step of faith, he will go before us and fight for us.

Prayer

Dear Lord, thank you for the promises you give us in your word. Thank you for your unfailing love and faithfulness. Please help me to have the courage to step out in faith and take possession of the things you have promised me.

Finding Joy: Give Generously

Day 29

"Give generously to them and do so without a grudging heart; then because of this the Lord your God will bless you in all your work and in everything you put your hand to"

—DEUT 15:10 NIV

"In everything I did, I showed you that by this kind of hard work we must help the weak, remembering the words the Lord Jesus himself said: 'It is more blessed to give than to receive'"

—ACTS 20:35 NIV

ALTHOUGH WE LIVE IN a prosperous nation, we are surrounded by people who are hurting financially, physically, mentally, and emotionally. As children of God, we should see the need that is around us and give generously to meet that need. Verse 8 above states, "be generous and lend them whatever they need." In the Old Testament, God established a system by which the Israelites' debts were canceled every seven years (see Deuteronomy 8:1–3), so when the Israelites lent money to a neighbor, they knew they might not ever receive it back. Yet God instructed them to give "generously" and "not grudgingly." That is a difficult thing to do in a world that is very materialistic. We are often socialized to hold onto money, save as much as possible, and build a future for ourselves and for our children. But the Bible teaches that when we give generously to others, he will bless us in all that we do. In other words, there is a promise of blessing when we give to others.

When we give generously to bless those around us, God, in turn, pours abundant blessings into our lives. His blessings are boundless. They may be in the form of financial blessings, good health, a well-adjusted family, a happy, fulfilling marriage, peace of mind, and on and on his blessings go.

But perhaps one of the greatest blessings we gain through giving is joy. When we sow seeds into the lives of others, there is an immediate reciprocal blessing of joy. It simply feels good to give to others, whether we give of our time, our abilities, or our finances (which could also be in the form of food, clothing, shelter, transportation, a job opportunity, or a baby shower for someone in need). God sees our willingness to bless others, and he in turn blesses us. This is not because of our goodness; it is because of his great love for us, and because he keeps his promises. If we have a willing heart, God will bring people into our lives, and he will prompt us as to what we should give and how much. There are often hurting people in our own families to whom we can give. God will show us what to do. He places that stirring in our spirit that cannot be ignored. He moves us with compassion, and he wants us to respond to that stirring by helping others. Holding on tightly to our resources seldom leads to happiness, and it often leads to misery. When we are obedient, we open up a channel for God's blessings to flow even more abundantly in our lives, and we experience true joy. (See also Prov 11:25 and Deut 16:17.)

Prayer

Dear Lord, thank you for the abundant blessings you have provided in my life. Please help me to be sensitive to your leading and to give generously to those people you place in my path. Help me to understand that giving to others increases my joy and brings me into closer fellowship with you.

Finding Joy: Live Harmoniously
Day 30

"Now may the God who gives perseverance and encouragement grant you to be of the same mind with one another according to Christ Jesus, so that with one accord you may with one voice glorify the God and Father of our Lord Jesus Christ. Therefore, accept one another, just as Christ also accepted us to the glory of God"

—ROM 15:5–7 NASB

MASTERING INTERPERSONAL RELATIONSHIPS CAN be challenging, even in the family of God, and opportunities for offense can arise almost daily in the workplace, at school, at church, and, especially, in one's own family unit and extended family. Sometimes the people we know the best and feel the closest to are able to hurt us the worst, perhaps because they know us so well. We often find it easier to be loving and gracious to strangers than to the people we rub shoulders with every day who may annoy us. God's word instructs us to live in harmony with each other. That includes the one who is difficult to love, the one who has wounded us, and the one who just gets under our skin. Proverbs 14:21 teaches that "it is a sin to despise one's neighbor" (NIV). Strife, contention, jealousy, envy, judgment and offense are tools of the enemy that distract us from our true purpose, which is to glorify God. We must take authority over those ungodly impulses and be a light to all those around us, even to our enemies.

Matthew 5:44 states, "But I say unto you, Love your enemies, bless them that curse you, do good to them that hate you, and pray for them which despitefully use you, and persecute you" (KJV).

When we feel those inner stirrings of negativity toward another human being, we need to remind ourselves of our own frailties and dependence on God. Often when we feel resentment, irritation or judgment toward another individual, it is not actually that person we are frustrated with as much as ourselves. Feelings of insecurity can be a trap that leads us to compare ourselves to others and inadvertently nurture seeds of jealousy, envy, and strife. We must stay full of the Holy Spirit, so that we are able to overcome those weaknesses of our sinful nature.

Proverbs 14:30 teaches us that, "A heart at peace gives life to the body, but envy rots the bones (NIV). Isn't that incredible? Our thought life is directly linked to our *physical* well being. When we can discipline ourselves to think and speak well of the people whom we find the most difficult to love, there is a reward and blessing for them and for us. Our purpose on this earth is to bring praise and glory to God. When we live in harmony with others, we are able to join our voices and hearts in unity and accomplish the work of his kingdom.

Prayer

Dear Lord, I confess my weakness in living in harmony with my fellow man. Please help me to speak well of others, to pray for those who falsely accuse me, and to love my neighbor as myself. I want to honor you in my personal relationships and love others with the love you have for me as much as is humanly possible. Please let my life and my relationships bring glory and praise to you.

Finding Joy: Love Abundantly
Day 31

"If I speak in the tongues of men or of angels, but do not have love, I am only a resounding gong or a clanging cymbal"

—1 COR 13:1 NIV

"Let love be your highest goal"

—1 COR 14:1 NIV

"And thou shalt love the Lord thy God with all thy heart, and with all thy soul, and with all thy mind, and with all thy strength: this is the first commandment. And the second is like, namely this, Thou shalt love thy neighbour as thyself. There is none other commandment greater than these"

—MARK 12:30-31 KJV

CLEARLY, IF WE ARE part of the family of God, loving others is of the utmost importance. God is love, and he wants us to demonstrate love to everyone around us, including ourselves (1 John 4:7–8). He tells us to love our neighbor as we love ourselves. How can we show love to others if we cannot even love who we are? The first step in loving is to appreciate the person God has made us to be and to be grateful for each day that he gives us. It is pretty easy to love our families and our close circle of friends, so we may think we're actually doing pretty well in this area, but God tells us that even the heathens love their friends (Luke 6:32–36). God teaches us to love our enemies. He wants us to love the unlovable. He wants us to love people who annoy us and frustrate us. He wants us to love the one who is an outcast, a criminal, a reprobate. God loves us all the same. It is not because of anything we have done that we belong to him; it is because of his great love for us, and everyone on Earth needs to know of that love (Eph. 2:4). We need to be the hands and feet of Jesus reaching out to others. We can demonstrate God's love to others through our words, our actions, our prayers, our kindness, our compassion, our willingness to share the message of the gospel, and our humility.

We, ourselves, are no better than the most wicked sinner. It is only the sacrifice of Christ and our acceptance of that precious gift that makes us worthy to come before him. We are surrounded by hurting people who need to see Christ's love demonstrated in our lives. People need to see a model of kindness, compassion, and caring. We cannot physically take people to Jesus, but we can show them Jesus through the love we share. When we are full of God's love, we are overflowing with joy and love for others. It is through that abundance that we can minister to others and, in return, we experience even more joy and fulfillment. I challenge us all to find ways to tangibly demonstrate God's love to everyone with whom we come in contact. "And now these three remain: faith, hope, and love. But the greatest of these is love" (1Cor. 13:13 NIV). (See also 1 John 4:18–20 and Matthew 22:34–40.)

Prayer

Dear Lord, thank you for loving me abundantly and unconditionally. Even when I have failed you, you have never stopped loving me. Now I pray that you will fill me with your Holy Spirit, and help me to demonstrate your love to *all* those around me. I forgive my enemies, and I pray that you would help me to demonstrate love to them as well. I surrender my selfish will to you, and I give you praise for your faithfulness and great mercy.

Final Thoughts

I PRAY THAT WE all continue in the faith, keep growing in spiritual wisdom, knowledge, and understanding, and faithfully fulfill the work God has called us to do. The apostle Paul says it best when he writes: "May the God of hope fill you with all joy and peace as you trust in him, so that you may overflow with hope by the power of the Holy Spirit" (Rom 15:13 NIV).

If you were touched in a positive way through this devotional, I would love to hear from you. Please feel free to contact me at: thereisbeautyhere@gmail.com

Blessings,
Rebecca

www.ingramcontent.com/pod-product-compliance
Lightning Source LLC
LaVergne TN
LVHW051707080426
835511LV00017B/2777